PAKISTAN

COUNTRIES IN CRISIS

ALAN WACHTEL

Rourke Publishing

www.rourkepublishing.com

PHOTO CREDITS: ARIF ALI/AFP/Getty Images: pp. 11, 35; Terry Ashe/Time Life Pictures/Getty Images:
p. 26; Bernard Bisson/Sygma/Corbis: p. 25; Margaret Bourke-White/Times Life Pictures/Getty Images:
p. 18; Getty Images: pp. 24, 37; ASIF HASSAN/AFP/Getty Images: p. 7; Aman Khan/istock: p. 19; Banaras
Khan/AFP/Getty Images: p. 40; Danish Khan/istock: p. 14; Saeed Khan/AFP/Getty Images: pp. 28, 31;
Library of Congress: pp. 13, 17; John Moore/Getty Images: p. 8; narvikk/istock: p. 29; Daniel Pearl Foundation:
p. 34; AAMIR QURESHI/AFP/Getty Images: pp. 5, 39; Christian Simonpietri/Sygma/Corbis: p. 22;
Ron Summers/istock: p. 21; Transport Security Administration: p. 32; U.S. Marine Corps: p. 33; Wojclech
Zwierzynski/istock: p. 12.

Cover picture shows supporters of opposition leader, Benazir Bhutto, during an anti-government protest in
November 2007. (Mohsin Raza/Reuters/Corbis)

Produced for Rourke Publishing by Discovery Books
Editor: Gill Humphrey
Designer: Keith Williams
Map: Stefan Chabluk
Photo researcher: Rachel Tisdale

Library of Congress Cataloging-in-Publication Data

Wachtel, Alan, 1968-
Pakistan / Alan Wachtel.
     p. cm. -- (Countries in crisis)
ISBN 978-1-60472-352-6
1. Pakistan--Juvenile literature. I. Title.
DS376.9.W33 2009
954.91--dc22

                              2008025141

Printed in the USA

CONTENTS

CHAPTER ONE

RETURN OF THE EXILES

In the fall of 2007, Pakistan's government was getting ready for elections. General Pervez Musharraf, the country's leader, wanted to run for re-election as president. Musharraf had taken power in 1999, when he led Pakistan's army in a military **coup**. In 2002, he also made himself Pakistan's president. Leading the army and being president made Musharraf very powerful.

Pakistan's **constitution** did not allow Musharraf to run for re-election as president while he also led the army. That law did not seem to stop Musharraf. He continued to run for re-election, with support from the Pakistan Muslim League-Q (PML-Q).

Pakistan's **Supreme Court** opposed Musharraf's wish to remain both president and head of the army. So did many of the country's politicians. One political party that was against Musharraf was the Pakistan People's Party (PPP), led by Benazir Bhutto. Another was the Pakistan Muslim League-N (PML-N), led by Nawaz Sharif. Although both of these parties were powerful in Pakistan, their leaders were living in **exile**. If they returned, they might face imprisonment.

As Pakistan prepared for elections, Musharraf had many of his opponents arrested, including some members of the Supreme Court. He also declared a **state of emergency** on

PAKISTAN

November 3, 2007. Musharraf said that he was tightening control of the country to make sure the election went smoothly and to prevent **terrorism**. Some people thought he was just trying to keep power for himself.

BHUTTO AND SHARIF COME HOME

Bhutto risked returning to Pakistan. On October 18, 2007, however, **suicide bombers** targeted her. They failed to kill Bhutto but did kill 134 others. Her freedom, however,

A protest in Islamabad in December, 2007. Lawyers and civil-rights activists march in support of Muneer Malik. Malik is one of the important lawyers in Pakistan who opposes Musharraf.

did not last long. Musharraf had her placed under house arrest on November 9. Sharif came back on November 17. He immediately demanded that Musharraf end the state of emergency and free the Supreme Court judges.

ASSASSINATION

Bhutto's house arrest was lifted on November 10, 2007. On December 27, 2007, she spoke at a rally in Rawalpindi. Bhutto was running for prime minister. The election was less than a month away, and she was one of the top candidates. As her limousine drove away from the rally, Bhutto stood up through the sunroof and waved to the crowd.

Former prime minister, Nawaz Sharif, gives a campaign speech in Sukkar in December, 2007.

Benazir Bhutto waves to a crowd at a campaign rally on December 27, 2007. Bhutto was assassinated later that day.

Then, gunshots rang out, and a suicide bomber blew himself up. Bhutto fell into the limousine. By the time the driver got her to a hospital, she was dead. No one knows whether she was killed by the bullets, the bomb, or a head injury as she tried to duck into the car. In addition, no one knew who sent the gunman and the suicide bomber to the rally.

PERVEZ MUSHARRAF

Pervez Musharraf was born in India in 1943, and came to Pakistan as a boy. He graduated from Pakistan's Military Academy in 1964, and he won a medal for fighting heroically in one of Pakistan's wars with India. By 1999, Musharraf was a top army general. When Prime Minister Nawaz Sharif tried to kick him out, Musharraf turned the tables on him and overthrew Sharif.

CRISIS IN PAKISTAN

From its founding in 1947, Pakistan has almost always been a country in crisis. The country has many problems, including terrorism, a **repressive** government, and a weak economy. Benazir Bhutto thought she could help solve some of these problems. Many people thought she was the only leader popular enough to win an election and bring reform to Pakistan. With Bhutto dead and Musharraf and Sharif wrestling for power, Pakistan's crises looked set to get worse.

CHAPTER TWO

LAND AND EARLY HISTORY

The modern nation of Pakistan is in Southwest Asia. It borders the Arabian Sea to the south, Iran to the west, India to the east, and Afghanistan to the northwest. The part of Kashmir that is controlled by Pakistan borders China. Today, Pakistan has more than 164 million people.

The country has three major geographical regions. Pakistan's northern highlands are part of the Himalayan mountain range, and the country includes the famous peaks K2 (28,251 feet or 8,611 meters) and Naga Parbat (26,660 feet or 8,126 meters).

WHERE IS PAKISTAN?

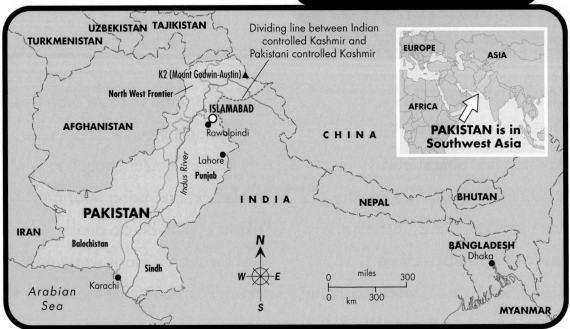

A Pakistani woman carries a box away from the remains of her house in Kashmir. Her home was destroyed by the powerful earthquake that hit Kashmir in October, 2005.

These mountains are among the highest, and most dangerous to climb, in the world. The Indus River plain contains some of Pakistan's best land for agriculture. It includes the provinces of Punjab and Sindh. The Balochistan Plateau is very dry, and has fewer people than anywhere else in Pakistan. In general, Pakistan's climate is dry, and there are sometimes droughts, but the country does have a rainy season from June through September. Pakistan also suffers from frequent earthquakes.

Naga Parbat is the second-highest mountain in Pakistan and the ninth-highest mountain in the world.

THE INDUS VALLEY CIVILIZATION

People first lived on the land that is now Pakistan thousands of years ago. The Indus Valley civilization, which lasted from 2500 BC to 1600 BC, was one of the earliest known human cultures.

Archaeologists have discovered cities, houses, and many artifacts from the Indus Valley civilization, but no one has yet been able to translate its writings.

THE VEDIC AGE

Historians are not sure how the

Indus Valley civilization ended. It may have been brought down by natural disasters, or conquered by invaders. Records of life in the Indus Valley from 1500 BC to 500 BC come from the *Vedas*, an ancient collection of **Hindu** hymns. The Vedas tell of people moving from the Indus Valley to the Ganges Valley (in modern India), and of the arrival of Hindu culture.

THE ARRIVAL OF ISLAM AND THE MUGHAL PERIOD

Muhammad bin Qasim, an explorer from Damascus, brought **Islam** to the regions of Balochistan and Sindh in AD 711. Over the next 1,000 years, Muslim rulers took over the area. The 1500s saw the rise

The Great Mosque of Wazir Khan stands in the city of Lahore. This photograph was taken at the end of the 19th century.

PAKISTANI FOOD

Meat, wheat, beans, and vegetables are staples of Pakistani food. *Chapatis* and *naan* are two types of bread that are popular in the country. Meats, including beef, chicken, and lamb, are often cooked on kebabs (sticks). Spicy dishes such as curries are also very popular. Different regions in Pakistan have different kinds of spices. For dessert, Pakistanis' can choose sweets such as *kulfi* and *gulab jamun*. *Chai*, or tea, is a popular drink.

Meat-and-vegetable kebabs are a popular meal in Pakistan.

of the Mughal Empire, when Islam became the region's main religion. During this period, European explorers arrived, and trade with Europe became a big business. The Mughal Empire lasted until the mid-1800s. As its power declined, the British East India Company gained control. At this time, the land that is now Pakistan was part of India.

BRITISH RULE

The British East India Company employed Muslim and Hindu soldiers in India. In 1857-1858, these soldiers rebelled. The soldiers thought the ammunition for the new weapons the British gave them was greased with pig or cow fat. This offended them because Muslims are not allowed to have contact with pigs, and cows are sacred to Hindus. After the British army put down the rebellion, Britain passed the Government of India Act of 1858. With this law, Britain ended the Mughal Empire for good and took control of the land that would eventually become the modern nations of India and Pakistan.

CHAPTER THREE

INDEPENDENT PAKISTAN

British rule of the region that became India and Pakistan was called the Raj. It contained large numbers of both Hindus and Muslims. Under the Raj, the land was known as British India. The Raj helped to develop the **infrastructure** and economy of the region. It did not, however, give the region's people a big role in government.

TOWARD INDEPENDENCE

In 1885, the Indian National Congress was formed to work for independence from Britain. Some Muslim leaders became afraid that if British India became independent, mostly Hindus would run it. One of these leaders was Mohammad Ali

This railway station is at Chaman, Pakistan. It is close to the Afghanistan border. When the British controlled the area they built a large network of railroads. This improved transportation across the region.

Jinnah. Jinnah was a member of the Indian National Congress until 1919.

WHAT'S IN A NAME?

In 1933, some students at Cambridge University, in Britain, wrote an essay called *Now or Never*. *Now or Never* promoted the idea of making part of British India into a Muslim country. One student came up with the name *Pakistan*. The country's name comes from the names of its regions: Punjab; Afghania, or North-West Frontier; Kashmir; and Indus-Sindh.

JINNAH'S ACHIEVEMENTS

" Few individuals significantly alter the course of history. Fewer still modify the map of the world. Hardly anyone can be credited with creating a nation-state. Mohammad Ali Jinnah did all three.

Quoted by biographer Stanley Wolpert.

"

He later joined the Muslim League, a group that worked for an

Indian Muslim leader Mohammad Ali Jinnah (right, holding a cigar). As head of the Muslim League, he declared the intention of creating Pakistan at a press conference in 1946.

independent Muslim country in British India. By 1940, Jinnah and the Muslim League were working to make an independent country out of the parts of northwestern and eastern British India that had a Muslim majority.

By the mid-1940s, British India was in crisis, with fierce riots and deadly massacres taking place. Britain knew it could not keep control of the country. Neither they nor the Hindus wanted to divide British India, but Jinnah and the Muslim League would not accept any other plan.

In the summer of 1947, Britain passed the India Independence Act. This act divided British India into the two countries of India and Pakistan. The Muslim-majority areas of Punjab and Bengal became part of Pakistan. Soon after, Sindh, Balochistan, and the North-West Frontier Province also joined Pakistan.

This division of the land became known as the Partition of India. The event led to a massive movement of people to the new countries, and outbreaks of rioting and violence. Many hundreds of thousands died and millions were made homeless as a result of the new boundaries.

TROUBLE WITH INDIA

As soon as it became independent, Pakistan faced a problem that continues to this day. The new countries of India and Pakistan could not agree about which of them should get Kashmir, a region to the east of the North-West Frontier Province. India and Pakistan fought wars over Kashmir in 1947 and 1965, and the threat of more violence over Kashmir is always there. When both countries gained nuclear weapons, the danger of the conflict increased further.

Many people think Kashmir is one of the most beautiful places in the world. The conflict between Pakistan and India over Kashmir, however, has made Kashmir a hard place to live.

POLITICS AND INSTABILITY

When Pakistan was founded, no one doubted who would lead it. Mohammad Ali Jinnah became the country's leader. Jinnah held this position until he died in 1948. After Jinnah's death, politics in Pakistan became complex, and often dangerous. Liaquat Ali Khan, who took over Jinnah's job, was assassinated in 1951. At times, Pakistan's army has taken over the country. In 1958, for example, General Mohammad Ayub Khan forced Pakistan's president Iskander Mirza out of power. In 1977, less than twenty years later, General Mohammad Zia ul-Haq removed Prime Minister Zulfikar Ali Bhutto (Benazir's father) from power.

EAST PAKISTAN BECOMES BANGLADESH

From 1947 to 1972, Pakistan was made up of East Pakistan and West Pakistan. In the early 1970s, conflict grew between East and West Pakistan. Each favored a different political party. The two parties could not work together to form one government for the country. When East Pakistan declared it would not pay taxes or obey the country's military government, the Pakistani army cracked down on it. Amid the violence, millions of refugees from East Pakistan flooded into India. India then invaded East Pakistan and defeated the Pakistani army. By early 1972, East Pakistan had become independent and had changed its name to Bangladesh.

Soldiers from India's army enter the city of Dhaka in 1971. With India's help, Dhaka became the capital of Bangladesh, formerly East Pakistan, after it split from Pakistan.

CHAPTER FOUR

THE BHUTTOS

Zulfikar Ali Bhutto, the leader of the Pakistan People's Party (PPP), was one of Pakistan's most popular leaders. He came to power in 1971, after President Agha Mohammad Yahya Khan resigned following the loss of East Pakistan. Bhutto was a powerful speaker, and his message of **socialism** appealed to many. Bhutto, however, failed to make many of the changes that he wanted. He also treated his opponents harshly.

Pakistani leader, Zulfikar Ali Bhutto, makes a speech at London Airport in 1973. He was unable to make changes in Pakistan, and was tried for murder and hanged in 1979.

President Mohammad Zia ul-Haq visits the presidential palace of France in October 1985. He was president of Pakistan until 1988 when he was killed in a plane crash.

In early 1977, Bhutto's PPP ran in an election against the Pakistan National Alliance (PNA). The PNA was a group of political parties that wanted Islam to play a bigger role in Pakistan's government.

When the PPP won the election, the PNA claimed the PPP had cheated. To control the protests, Bhutto declared **martial law**. General Mohammad Zia ul-Haq took charge of the country.

ZIA

Zia soon had Bhutto arrested for attempted murder, and the former leader was tried and sentenced to death. Zulfikar Ali Bhutto was hanged on April 4, 1979. Zia also Islamized the country. He set up courts to hear cases and punish people according to Islamic law. Zia remained in control of Pakistan until 1988, longer than any other leader. His rule may have lasted longer, but he and his top generals were all killed in a plane crash on August 17, 1988. The plane crash was no accident. Investigators found that it was the result of "a criminal act of **sabotage** perpetrated in the aircraft."

BENAZIR

Pakistan's 1988 election was historic. Benazir Bhutto succeeded in bringing the PPP back to life.

Prime Minister Benazir Bhutto gives a speech to the United States Congress on June 1, 1989.

BENAZIR BHUTTO

> She is part Radcliffe and Oxford [British college and university], with an extremely well-stocked mind, full of feminist literature, peace marches, the Oxford Union, and with a very liberated social life. She is also. . .the daughter and granddaughter of immensely wealthy landlords, whose inheritance gave her the right to rule. . .And she is also part of a. . .myth: of a populist father. . .who was overthrown by a usurper [someone who takes over a position of power by force] and killed. . .and of the slip of a girl who, after a decade of imprisonment and struggle routed [defeated] her father's enemies to become prime minister.
>
> *Extract from* Pakistan: In the Shadow of Jihad and Afghanistan, *by Mary Anne Weaver.*

Benazir's victory made her the world's first female leader of an Islamic country. She was unable, however, to bring about many of the changes she promised. Worse, Benazir became known for giving government jobs to members of her family and for firing government officials who had disagreed with her father. She lost power in 1990 but regained it in 1993. In 1996, however, she again lost power as a result of money problems and **corruption**. In 1999, she was convicted of corruption and exiled from Pakistan.

SHARIF AND THE BOMB

Benazir Bhutto's main rival, Nawaz Sharif, won Pakistan's 1997 election. During Sharif's rule, Pakistan joined the small group of countries armed with nuclear weapons. In response to nuclear-weapons testing by India, Pakistan tested nuclear bombs of its own. Pakistan's nuclear tests harmed its

Pakistan tested its nuclear weapons under this hill in the province of Balochistan. Standing in front of the hill are Dr. Samar Mubarak (right) and Dr. Ishfaq Ahmed (left), both leading scientists in Pakistan, and Pakistan's Minister of Information, Musahid Hussain.

relations with the United States. After the tests, the United States put economic **sanctions** on Pakistan and refused to sell it weapons.

REACTIONS TO PAKISTAN'S NUCLEAR TEST

"Recent nuclear tests by India and Pakistan and the resulting increase in tension between them, are a source of deep and lasting concern to both [the United States and China]. . . .Our shared interests in a peaceful and stable South Asia and in a strong global nonproliferation regime [limiting the production of nuclear weapons] have been put at risk by these tests, which we have joined in condemning."

From U.S president Bill Clinton's speech against the testing of nuclear weapons by India and Pakistan, June 27, 1998.

The border between India and Pakistan has been a flashpoint of conflict for decades. Many people fear nuclear war between the two countries.

CHAPTER FIVE

THE MUSHARRAF YEARS

In October 1999, a struggle for power took place in Pakistan. Nawaz Sharif, Pakistan's prime minister, plotted to gain more power for himself. He tried to replace the country's top army general, General Pervez Musharraf, with another man. On October 12, Sharif introduced the man he wanted to be top general to other Pakistani generals. The Pakistani generals, however, were loyal to Musharraf. Instead of agreeing to Sharif's proposal, they arrested him.

While this was happening, Musharraf was on a flight from Sri Lanka back to Pakistan. The pilot reported that his plane, which was carrying Musharraf and almost 200 other passengers, was not being allowed to land in Pakistan. Sharif had given orders he hoped would force Musharraf's flight to land in enemy territory. At the last minute, Musharraf's men told the airport officials what was happening. They then allowed Musharraf's plane to land in Pakistan, just before it ran out of fuel. When Musharraf stepped off the plane, he was the new leader of Pakistan.

HUNTING AL-QAEDA

Since 1996, Pakistan supported the Taliban, the **Islamist** group that ruled Afghanistan and sheltered the terrorist leader Osama bin Laden.

General Pervez Musharraf speaks to reporters after taking over Pakistan's government in a military coup in 1999.

The ruins of the World Trade Center after the September 11, 2001 terrorist attacks on the United States. These attacks forced U.S. leaders to pay close attention to Pakistan. Pakistan borders Afghanistan, the country that sheltered al-Qaeda.

Pakistan and Afghanistan are neighbors, and many Pakistanis support the Taliban. Musharraf had resisted U.S. pressure to fight the Taliban and catch Osama bin Laden.

Everything changed when bin Laden's group, al-Qaeda, struck the United States on September 11, 2001. Since then, Pakistan has been among the **allies** of the United States in the fight against al-Qaeda. Khalid Sheikh Mohammed, the al-Qaeda leader who is said to have planned the September 11 attacks, was captured in Pakistan in 2003. In 2006, the United States bombed a party in Damadola, Pakistan in an attempt to kill Ayman al-Zawahiri, a major al-Qaeda leader. The attack caused outrage in Pakistan, and it did not kill Zawahiri.

SELLING NUCLEAR SECRETS

A.Q. Khan is famous in Pakistan as the father of the country's nuclear program. In 2003, Italian coast guard patrols got a tip from the CIA and MI6 (intelligence services of the United States and Britain) and stopped a ship called the *BBC China*. They found that it was loaded with equipment for making nuclear fuel. The shipment came from a network run by Khan.

A **propaganda** poster of Osama bin Laden the leader of al-Qaeda, the terrorist group that carried out the September 11, 2001 attacks on the United States. Bin Laden is among the most wanted men in the world. Some people believe he might be living in a remote area of Pakistan.

THE MURDER OF DANIEL PEARL

Daniel Pearl was a reporter who worked for the *Wall Street Journal*. In early 2002, he was in Karachi, Pakistan, working on a story. When Pearl disappeared on January 23, 2002, many peopled feared the worst. Pearl had been kidnapped by members of al-Qaeda and murdered. Khalid Sheikh Mohammed said he committed the murder.

Wall Street Journal reporter Daniel Pearl was murdered by al-Qaeda members while working in Pakistan in 2002.

Pakistan's top nuclear scientist was selling nuclear secrets! A spy found that Khan had been dealing with countries such as Libya and Iran. In 2004, Khan confessed on TV to running the network. The next day, Musharraf pardoned him. This event led many people to believe that Pakistan was not a safe country to have nuclear weapons.

MUKHTAR MAI AND WOMEN'S RIGHTS

In 2002, Mukhtar Mai was raped as part of a punishment for a wrong committed by her brother. Although the rape was ordered by the elders of her small village, Mai brought charges against the men who raped her. The case went to Pakistan's highest court. The rapists were found guilty. Mai used the money she won in court to set up schools in her village. She says, "I have a message to the women of the world and all the women who have been raped or any [other] kind of violation: that, no matter what, they must talk about it and they must fight for justice."

Mukhtar Mai works to educate girls in Pakistan. Mai thinks that educating girls in Pakistan will help to reduce violence against women in the country.

CHAPTER SIX

A DANGEROUS PLACE

In early 2008, *The Economist*, an important news magazine, called Pakistan "the world's most dangerous place." One threat to Pakistan is the spread of the Taliban into the country. After September 11, 2001, Musharraf claimed that Pakistan would no longer support the Taliban. In spite of this, many news reports say that the Taliban has a lot of support from Pakistan's people. Some fear that the Taliban, or even al-Qaeda, could destabilize Pakistan and possibly get a nuclear weapon.

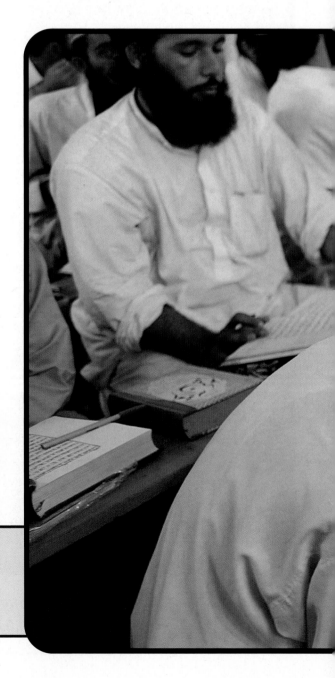

Pakistan has many madrassas, or Islamic religious schools. Some of these schools have a reputation for promoting radical versions of Islam.

PAKISTAN

WHO KILLED BENAZIR BHUTTO?

Benazir Bhutto claimed not to fear death, although she knew she might be a target for assassins. Pakistan's government quickly blamed the October 18 bombing that narrowly missed Bhutto and the December 27 bombing that killed her on al-Qaeda. Bhutto herself feared Islamists within the government more than al-Qaeda. Before she returned to Pakistan, Bhutto even sent a letter to Musharraf naming government officials who might want to kill her. In March 2008, Pakistan's police accused Baitullah Mehsud, a terrorist leader, of plotting Bhutto's assassination.

THE FUTURE OF THE PPP

After Benazir Bhutto's assassination, her husband and her son took over leadership of

BAITULLAH MEHSUD

Baitullah Mehsud is the young and mysterious leader of a terrorist group in Pakistan called Tehrik-e-Taliban. Little is known about him, and his face has never been photographed. His group is said to be behind more than sixty suicide bombings that have killed hundreds of people, including the attack that killed Benazir Bhutto. Pakistan's government claims it listened in to Mehsud saying to another militant, "Fantastic job. Very brave boys, the ones who killed her," after Bhutto's murder.

the PPP. Their only qualifications are their connections to Benazir. Bhutto's husband, Asif Ali Zardari, is a businessman who already has a reputation for corruption.

On December 30, 2007, father and son Asif Ali Zardari and Bilawal Bhutto Zardari, announced that they would lead the Pakistan People's Party (PPP) after Benazir Bhutto's assassination. Asif was the slain leader's husband. Bilawal is their son.

Her son, Bilawal, is a nineteen-year-old college student. Zardari says he plans to keep the party together until Bilawal is prepared to lead it.

In January 2008, Pakistani lawyer Ali Ahmed Kurd and his children give a victory sign to a group of lawyers protesting Musharraf's firing of the head of Pakistan's Supreme Court. Kurd is being held under house arrest.

CAN MUSHARRAF RUN?

In January 2008, one of the Supreme Court judges removed by Musharraf sent a letter to major leaders in the United States and Europe. "There can be no democracy without an independent judiciary, and there can be no independent judge in Pakistan until the action of November 3 is reversed," said Iftikhar Muhammad Chaudhry. Even though Musharraf stepped down from Pakistan's military, Chaudhry still wants Pakistan's Supreme Court to decide whether Musharraf can run for president. Chaudhry could not send the letter himself because Pakistan's government keeps him confined to his house. His teenage daughter smuggled the letter out of the country for him.

ELECTIONS

Pakistan held parliamentary elections in February 2008. Benazir Bhutto's party, the Pakistan People's Party (PPP), and Nawaz Sharif's party, the Pakistan Muslim League-N, both gained many seats in the country's parliament. Musharraf's party, the Pakistan Muslim League-Q (PML-Q), was the big loser. Both the PPP and the PML-N oppose Musharraf. Musharraf looked likely to lose much of his remaining power, but some worried that he may try to hold on to power by dissolving the country's parliament.

Pakistan faces many challenges, including its leadership crisis and the threat from the Taliban and al-Qaeda. How the country handles these problems will affect Pakistan's future stability and its role in the world.

Voters in Balochistan stand in line to cast their ballots on February 18, 2008. The voters were choosing members for the country's parliament. Many people did not vote because they feared polling stations would be attacked by suicide bombers.

TIMELINE

BC

ca. 2500-1600 Indus Valley civilization

ca. 1500-500 Vedic Age

AD

711 Muhammad bin Qasim brings Islam to Balochistan and Sindh.

1526 Mughal Empire begins.

1707-1858 Mughal Empire declines.

1858 Britain passes the Government of India Act, creating British India.

1885 Indian National Congress forms.

1906 Muslim League forms.

1940 Muslim League begins working for a separate Muslim nation.

1947 Britain passes the India Independence Act; Pakistan becomes independent.

1971 Civil war between East Pakistan and West Pakistan; Zulfikar Ali Bhutto becomes president.

1972 East Pakistan becomes Bangladesh.

1977 General Mohammad Zia ul-Haq overthrows Bhutto.

1979 Zulfikar Ali Bhutto executed.

1988 Benazir Bhutto is elected prime minister.

1990 Nawaz Sharif is elected prime minister.

1993 Sharif loses power; Benazir Bhutto returns as prime minister.

1996 Benazir Bhutto loses power; Pakistan begins supporting the Taliban in Afghanistan.

1999 Benazir Bhutto is convicted of corruption and exiled; General Pervez Musharraf overthrows Sharif in a military coup.

2001 Terrorist attacks by al-Qaeda in the United States; United States and an international coalition invade Afghanistan; Pakistan sides with the United States.

2002 American reporter Daniel Pearl murdered in Pakistan by al-Qaeda.

2007 Benazir Bhutto is assassinated.

2008 Elections held. Musharraf's party loses many seats in Parliament. A new prime minister, Yousuf Raza Gilani, is elected.

PAKISTAN

GEOGRAPHY

Area: 307,374 square miles (796,095 sq km)—excluding Pakistan-administered Kashmir

Borders: Afghanistan, China, India, Iran

Terrain: Flat Indus plain in the east, mountains in the north and northwest, and the Balochistan plateau in the west

Highest point: K2 (Mount Godwin-Austin) 28,251 feet (8,611 meters)

Resources: Natural gas, coal, iron ore, copper, salt, limestone, limited oil

Major rivers: Indus, Jhelum, Chenab, Ravi, Sutlej, Beas

SOCIETY

Population (2007): 164,741,924

Ethnic groups: Punjabi, Sindhi, Pashtun, Baloch, Muhajir

Languages: Punjabi, Sindhi, Siraiki, Pashtu, Urdu (official), Balochi, Hindko, Brahui, English, Burushaski, and others   **Literacy:** 77%

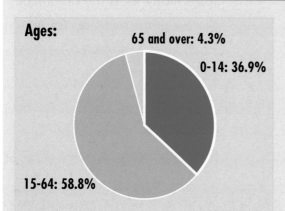

Ages:
65 and over: 4.3%
0-14: 36.9%
15-64: 58.8%

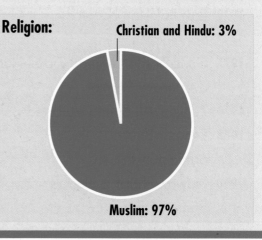

Religion:
Christian and Hindu: 3%
Muslim: 97%

GOVERNMENT

Type: Federal republic

Capital: Islamabad **Provinces**: 4, 1 territory, 1 capital territory

Independence: August 14, 1947

Law: Based on English common law, and Islamic law

Vote: Universal—18 years of age

System: President (chief of state); head of government (prime minister); Senate,100 seats (elected for six-year term), National Assembly, 342 seats (elected for 5-year term)

ECONOMY

Currency: Pak rupee **Labor force (2006):** 49.18 million

Total value of goods and services (2007): $446.1 billion

Poverty: 24% of people below poverty line

Main industries: textiles and clothing, food processing, pharmaceuticals, construction materials, paper products, fertilizer, shrimp

Foreign debt (2006/7): $38 billion

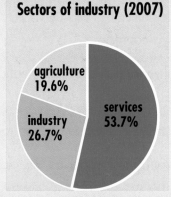

Sectors of industry (2007)

agriculture 19.6%

industry 26.7%

services 53.7%

COMMUNICATIONS AND MEDIA

Telephones (2006): 5.24 million fixed line; 63.16 million mobile (2007)

Internet users (2006): 12 million **TV stations (2006):** 20 stations (5 state-run channels, 15 privately-owned satellite channels) **Newspapers:** about 9 national daily papers and two weeklies. Printed in English or Urdu **Radio:** Radio Pakistan—state-run with 25 stations nationwide; 2 private music stations

Airports: 14 **Railroads:** 5,072 miles (8,163 km) **Roads:** 103,859 miles (167,146 km)

Ships: 14 over 1,000 tons **Ports:** Karachi, Port Muhammad Bin Quasim

MILITARY

Branches: Army, navy, air force

Service: voluntary military service at age 16; soldiers cannot be used in combat until age 18

GLOSSARY

allies (AL-lize): countries that support each other

archaeologists (ar-kee-OL-uh-jist): a person who studies the past by digging up old buildings or remains

constitution (kon-stuh-TOO-shuhn): the basic laws of a country

corruption (kuh-RUHP-shuhn): behavior that is dishonest

coup (KOO): a sudden action to win power

exile (EG-zile): a period of time during which a person is forced to live outside his or her home country

Hindu (HIN-doo): connected to the Indian religion of Hinduism

infrastructure (IN-fru-struhk-chur): basic utilities of a city or country, such as road, power, and water systems

Islam (ISS luhm): religion based on the teachings of the Prophet Muhammad. Followers of the religion are called Muslims.

Islamist (ISS-luhm-ist): a person who wants society to be run according to the laws of Islam

martial law (MAR shuhl LAW): government of a country by the military

propaganda (prop uh GAN duh): information spread to influence the way people think. Propaganda often gives an unfair or one-sided view.

repressive (ri-PRESS-if): using force to prevent people from expressing themselves

sabotage (SAB-uh-tahzh): harm done by an enemy agent to a nation's property

sanctions (SANGK shuhns): actions taken against a nation thought to have broken international law. For example refusing to trade with it.

socialism (SOH-shuh-liz-uhm): a political system where wealth is shared equally between people, and the main industries are owned by the government

state of emergency (STATE OV i-MUR-juhn-see): a period of time in which a country's government gives itself special powers to deal with a problem

suicide bomber (SOO-uh-side BOM-ur): a terrorist who explodes a bomb attached to his or her body

Supreme Court (suh-PREEM KORT): the highest court in a state or country

terrorism (TER-ur-iz-uhm): use of violence to scare people into giving in to political demands

FURTHER INFORMATION

WEBSITES

BBC News Country Profile: Pakistan

news.bbc.co.uk/1/hi/world/south_asia/
country_profiles/1157960.stm
*This site has the latest news, a timeline,
a country profile, and links.*

CIA World Factbook: Pakistan

www.cia.gov/library/publications/
the-world-factbook/geos/pk.html
The site has facts and statistics on Pakistan.

CNN.com: 100 Stories on Pakistan

topics.edition.cnn.com/topics/pakistan
*This site has some of the latest news stories
from Pakistan.*

Exploring Pakistan

www.geographia.com/pakistan/pak02.htm
*The site gives interesting information on
the geography of Pakistan.*

UNESCO World Heritage Center –
Pakistan

http://whc.unesco.org/en/statesparties/pk
*This site has lots of information on important
cultural and historical sites in Pakistan.*

BOOKS

Pakistan (Modern World Nations series).
Samuel Willard Crompton, Chelsea House
Publications, 2006.

Pakistan (Countries & Cultures series). Marc
Tyler Nobleman, Capstone Press, 2006.

Suicide Bombers (Fighting Terrorism series).
David Baker, Rourke Publishing, 2006.

INDEX